HOW TO BECOME AN
UNSTOPPABLE
Black Woman

5 *Steps*
to a positive image in a sea of negative stereotypes

Ms. Crystal Figueroa,

Reach for your dreams and sail on your own star! There are no limits, so..... Be unstoppable!

Love,
Tamlyn L. Franklin

TAMLYN L. FRANKLIN

How To Become An UNSTOPPABLE Black Woman
©2016 Tamlyn L. Franklin

ISBN: 978-0692619520

All rights reserved. No part of this publication may be reproduced or transmitted in any form or by any means, electronic or mechanical, including photocopying, recording, or by any information storage and retrieval system, without the prior written permission from the author, except where permitted by law. Contact the author for information on foreign rights.

Printed in the United States of America

Acknowledgements

It takes a village to raise a child. And it takes a great support system to accomplish some of life's goals. My support system is far reaching, and this book could not have been completed without the help of some great people in my life.

First, I'm thankful to God, the Creator for blessing me with the idea to write about what has been on my mind and heart for some time. I'm also grateful for the connections I've made in my life because of divine intervention. Thank you God for everything!

A very special thank you to my dear friend, Kimmoly, for posting a Facebook invitation for the Ready to Write Boot Camp. I love you, girl.

Special thanks to Towanda for your editing revisions and tireless efforts.

Carolyn, thank you for the book layout and cover design.

To my sister Gwen, who's my sounding board, walking partner, soul sister who finishes my sentences, main apple scrapple, travel buddy, and so much more. I love you, my sister!

Thank you to my girlfriends who inspire, encourage, uplift, who are honest, and provide a listening ear when a sister needs to vent. I'm thankful for our walks and talks, the tears we've cried and, the laughs we've shared making memories that will forever live in my heart. Thank you to my girls Kath, Lynn, Lisa, Rhonda, Censeria, and a special thank you to Robyn for your work (The Best of Reclaiming Kin). When you shine, you give others (me) permission to shine. You make this journey called life interesting and fun.

Thank you to my family, especially my children and grandchildren. I love you all to the moon and back.

To my husband, who's my lover and my friend. I thank you being in my corner, having my back, bearing with me during the writing of this book, and standing in the gap when I'm inaccessible due to this mission. I appreciate you. I value your counsel. I honor and cherish our marriage. I love you, forever.

Table of Contents

Foreword *vi*

Introduction *viii*

Chapter One
I Got You! 6

Chapter Two
Embrace Your Beauty 21

Chapter Three
Cherish Your Femininity 39

Chapter Four
Forgive To Be Forgiven 59

Chapter Five
Never Give Up 87

Notes 103

Foreword

What an exhilarating joy to read a piece of work filled with such raw emotion and love for my sisters, black women. The ebb and flow, and poetic nature of this brilliant writing put me in the mindset of the greats that have gone on before us. Oh how proud they must be that someone is bold enough to speak the truth in love, for such a time as this.

Calling for transparency, change, commitment and courage from what seems like a dying breed. I'd imagine the words of this book will hurt first and heal second. I commend Tamlyn Franklin for letting her passion hit the page in such a bold and courageous way. I know all who dare to read beyond page one, putting offense aside, will be forever changed and challenged to do better, live stronger, and show up beautiful in every shape, form, shade, and syllable of their lives. The words will challenge some and confirm for others what they already know to be true. We are being called higher. No longer can we confirm for media and society that every black woman is thirsty, vain, undervalued, loud, angry, and hateful toward one another. The time is now. It has been written, I dare you to read, learn, grow, and love.

Kimmoly Rice-Ogletree
Author, "Principles of the Ultimate Business Diva"
www.successcoachkimmoly.com

Introduction

This book is for black women and black girls. I'm unmistakably and unapologetically black. I love all people and all races. However, I'm not ashamed of my race. I love black people because we are an exceptional race. Some may wonder why black people are exceptional: It's because everything that black people have built, initiated, excelled at, overcame, and became is oftentimes hidden, stolen, or rewritten to benefit someone else. Black people have been minimized, marginalized, excluded, exploited, and classified as a "minority," disenfranchised, or systematically discriminated against or simply lumped together as the "people of color" category, ignored and forgotten. Blacks are the only people on the planet who were, for the most part, shipped to this country. Other races either migrated to America or died desperately trying to get here.

Historically, black people have been unfairly broad-brushed—labeled by a few influential folk as being: subpar educated, law breakers, violent criminals, athletic, lazy, and crazy. We know all of these labels are far from the truth.

Unfortunately, black women receive their own separate labels: aggressive, belligerent, or angry, just to name a few. These negative classifications have purposely tarnished our image. It's time to flip the script and work to change our position. We can change the world's perception of the black race starting with black women. We can put a positive spin on the ostensible negative image that is accepted as truth by many.

It is my hope that every black man, woman, and child reject mediocre labels and change any indecent behavior in our community. We can do whatever it takes to unite and uplift each other to reclaim, substantiate, and seal our original image as exceptional people we were created to be.

"Never doubt that a small group of committed citizens can change the world, truly it's the only thing that ever has," said American cultural anthropologist Margaret Mead. In other words, if I lock arms with you, and you lock arms with the black woman next to you, and we lock arms with every black person in our community, we can move forward as strong black people. The time is now. Let's be relentless in our personal endeavors. Let's be unified in community efforts. Let's reclaim our image, ourselves.

While I cannot single-handedly fix the race problem, I can help open the eyes of black girls and women to encourage them to stand tall and be proud of their complexions and ancestors. No matter your shade of brownness, you can speak up for what is right, cherish your femininity, and never shrink back when competing for something. Never quit, and always fight for your dreams and your community to simply be UNSTOPPABLE.

As you turn the page, a letter awaits you. In fact, a personal letter introduces each chapter. Moreover, my letter to the black man turned out to be the catalyst in writing this book.

Dear Sisters:

May I have your ear for a minute—or for the rest of our years? Yes, all of you, my beautiful black sisters, those who were blessed with an ample dose of melanin, those who received a tiny sprinkle, and all those who fall within the lines of the beautiful brown spectrum. We are sisters, beautiful black sisters.

When I extend my plate of life to offer you a kind smile, a warm greeting, a welcome conversation, or an opportunity for fellowship, you glaringly look me up and down and scream with your eyes "WHAT ARE YOU LOOKING AT?"

Please know I don't want to fight with you, so I turn and walk away. I see you're on the defense, guarding your heart. Don't you recognize me? Don't you remember the day we arrived here from the same soil, from our distant homeland?

We are forever sisters. We merely come from different mothers: black ones, white ones, and ones classified as other. You mean we can't even acknowledge one another as we walk the streets? Why my dear? Is it my skin tone you despise? Or maybe it's the car I drive? Maybe it's the style or the length of my hair, or could it be the tawdry clothes I wear?

Did you buy the lies that put us in opposing corners where we still stand, at the ready, to fight or kill, to this very day? Maybe you bought the lies that caused us to be at war with one another from the word "go" and even more so after the birth and death of Jim Crow.

Will we ever open our eyes? Will we ever refuse the daily dose of insecurities served in every flavor, to our liking, by almost every media entity? When will we distinguish the truth from the lies? And realize that we were the pawns in a game some thinking we were queens not realizing that we were all the same. Is it something in me that is causing this enmity or is it your insecurity that has been ingrained in your very being?

It saddens me that we continue this madness after centuries of suffering—not just me, not just you—but every person with a brown hue. I don't hate you, my sister, I understand you were trying to survive. But, so was I….So was I.

In peace and love,

Your black sister (I come in every shade of brown)

Chapter One
I Got You!

"Hello," I answer my phone at 7 a.m. catching my breath getting ready for work. My sister, Gwen, whispers, "Tam, you have a minute?" Immediately, I sensed distress in her voice. "I will make one," I quickly shot back.

"You can count on me through thick and thin, a friendship that will never end, when you are weak, I will be strong, helping you to carry on, call on me, I will be there, don't be afraid, please believe me when I say, count on me."

"Girl, can you talk?" "Are you sitting down?" "Are you ready for this?" These questions come without any warning. As women, we go through so many life changes that we just need to know that someone is genuinely in our corner.

As the sole provider for her family, Gwen was feeling the pressures to make her monthly sale quotas. She needed a friendly reminder that God had not brought her this far to leave her now, with no referrals. I boldly proclaimed, "The God that *I* serve created the entire universe and has all power and has total control over everything. Surely, he could open a door, window, or the heavens to pour out the referrals you need to meet your quota."

Shortly after our conversation, Gwen made her monthly quota and to day continues to meet her quarterly sales quotas.

AN EXTRA DOSE OF CARE

Oftentimes women simply need assurance and genuine support from a friend or loved one telling them that everything will be all right. Genuine support may take on numerous forms: a phone call to assure her that everything will work together for the better; a listening ear; a hand to hold during a difficult situation; a hand to squeeze during a joyful event; or your presence (to sit with you in silence).

We need to feel the support and know we can rejoice about life accomplishments for friends, family, or strangers. Whether it's a job promotion, a new business opportunity, or a never-married girlfriend meeting the man of our dreams, without hating.

Why can't women share good news such as about buying a new car or going on an all-paid exclusive island vacation without someone hating on us?

Women want to share their desires, frustrations, or challenges without their business spreading quicker than a social media update. Whether we discuss issues about our children, a spouse, a boss, or a coworker, share juicy information, or reveal goals, ideas, and dreams, we don't want to be judged or criticized.

We should be able to leave our purse, wallet, or our man in the same room with you and not have to worry about our possessions or honey being stolen (*you know some women can be scandalous*).

SOLID FRIENDSHIPS KEEP YOU SANE

A solid friendship helps strengthen your faith and gives you a reason not to quit on yourself, your family, or your dreams.

Let's say you got fired from you job—with no warning. You'd likely need someone to talk to keep you from losing your cool, your faith, or your freedom (law enforcers have no problem locking up disorderly and peaceful people).

What if your husband of 15 years, comes home, packs his suitcase, and drops the ball telling you he doesn't want to be married any longer, a true friend can keep you sane.

Sisterhood is a special kind of friendship between sisters (women from the same or another mother). The lyrics at the beginning of this chapter are from "Count on Me" by Whitney Houston and

CeCe Winans from the movie "Waiting to Exhale." a song from the movie, "Waiting to Exhale." We can't forget about the rapper Whodini, who poetically illustrates in his song Friends that "a friend is somebody you judge for yourself, some are okay and treat you real cool, and some mistake your kindness for a being a fool."

THE SEVEN Cs OF A FRIENDSHIP

A friendship could last four years or a lifetime.

I refer to seven elements that can identify a friendship: commitment, compassion, compunction, compromise, cheerleaders, constructive, and compatibility. With help from *Merriam Webster's Dictionary*[1], following are the definitions:

COMMITMENT

The state of being emotionally or intellectually devoted.

Every relationship has peaks and valleys, scuffs, bumps, and disagreements; if it didn't, then it would be perfect, and no relationship is perfect because no human being is perfect.

My siblings and I typically celebrate our birthdays privately, with a cake, sometimes a special dinner with a few friends and/or family members. We rarely, if ever, have birthday parties. I surprised my sister with her very first birthday party when she turned 50. I had a guest list of 75 people, which included family, her friends and coworkers, and a few of my closest friends since they've known her more than half their lives. I loved seeing my sister cry tears of joy seeing all the smiling faces at her birthday party, especially childhood friends.

But I was a little disappointed when my dear sister-friend, Censeria, didn't show up. I was mad and felt she should have been at my sister's birthday party no matter what, but deep down inside, I knew something serious could have happened. Later that day Censeria called me to give her regrets and let me know that she was going through a serious situation at home. I was heartbroken about her situation, but relieved we talked and told her there was no need to apologize.

COMPASSION

A deep awareness of the suffering of another accompanied by the wish to relieve it.

When your friend is going through an overwhelming life event such as the loss of a job or someone important to her, you may not fully understand what she's going through, but you can certainly feel your friend's pain so much that you just wish there was something, anything you could do to ease her pain. True friendship has an element of compassion.

COMPUNCTION
Feeling genuine remorse, guilt, or regret.

If a friend asked you to attend a special event and you couldn't make it because of a conflict, then you would feel remorse. But, true friendship means that your friend would feel a sense of guilt and pain she may have caused you. Likewise, your disappointed friend would feel the pain of her friend and would do what she could to relieve it based on the previous element, compassion. Your friend would do what she could to relieve your pain by being compassionate and forgive her friend's infraction.

COMPROMISE
A settlement of differences in which each side makes concessions.

Compromise means that the relationship is balanced. Both people give and take and make concessions for the other. If two people go out to eat together every Friday to end the work week, then they will likely alternate choosing the restaurant. If, it's always "her way or the highway," then that's not compromise, it's selfishness, not friendship.

CHEERLEADER
One who expresses praise for or promotes something enthusiastically.

Friendship means there is **cheerleader** or a strong supporter in the relationship, either or both. A friend who shares an idea with a friend about her desire to start a business will be encouraged and supported by her friend. However, if the friend does not show support because she's envious, jealous, or hopes her friend is unsuccessful in her endeavor or fails, then she may be a frenemy, not a friend. A frenemy is an enemy disguised as a friend – you know, a proverbial wolf in sheep's clothing. Don't waste time with so called friends who do not genuinely support you.

CONSTRUCTIVE (CRITICISM)
Serving to build or improve.

A true friend will tell you the truth, in love, and provide constructive feedback about things that they may see from a different vantage point. At times one friend can stand in the middle of the picture, but can't see the frame. The other friend, who is able to see her friend, the frame, the picture, and everything surrounding the picture, can offer advice or constructive criticism that could help her friend. A friend will not tell you the truth to hurt you, but will tell you the truth to protect you from the danger that you may not see, at the time.

COMPATIBILITY
Able to exist together harmoniously.

A good friendship is when people share common interests or tastes. However, if there is no harmony, no unity, no common interests, and combativeness, then either person may be described as something other than a friend, possibly a foe. If a relationship is filled with constant bickering, causes distress, stress and anxiety, and negatively affects one or both parties' physical mental or emotional health, then it may be described as dysfunctional and could mean that it's time to move on.

Supporting another person takes time, energy and resources. So take the time to listen to and genuinely help a sister in need. Many times the sister who may be standing in need of support is the one in the mirror: YOU. Support and show love to your sister friends. Don't "hate on" (wish the worse) friends because they may have someone special with whom they can share life and you don't; or they have a position you want; or they possess things (home, car, children, money) that you think you should have, etc. Rejoice with other women. Treat them the way you would have them treat you if the roles were reversed.

Be the kind of friend who, regardless how crazy, ridiculous, and silly a request may be, your friend can count on you to listen. No matter how many times a friend recites a life event that has caused her deep pain and shares stories about wounds that are slow to heal, provide a safe place for her to vent. When you see or talk with that friend, show her love. She will feel the warmth, genuine concern, and well wishes that you shower on her (and vice versa).

MOTHERLY WISDOM

My mom shared sage advice with me several months ago (I love our midnight chats): "Tam, when friends dwindle and drift out of your life or out of your circle, just know that **The Lord** has moved them out. Don't try to bring them back. If they come back to the circle on their own, then keep them. However, if they come back to the circle and you feel that it is forced or insincere, let them go. Don't waste energy trying to figure out what happened. It's okay to let people go. It's okay to build new friendship circles. Some people are only in your life for a season, a specific reason, or a lifetime." I listened to mom and told her that I firmly believe that whenever you lose one friend, you always gain two.

When you genuinely support other women, there is no doubt that other women will support you. Iron sharpens iron, and one man (woman) sharpens another. This means that when iron blades are rubbed together, each becomes sharper and more effective. Likewise, when friends are involved in one another's lives, mutual edification occurs. So, as you wish that others would do to you, do so to them. Be the kind of friend that you want in your circle. When you sow seeds of goodness, you will reap a harvest of goodness.

Exercise:

Examine your circle of friends. List your closest friends. Now determine if the people who you call friends are true friends. If not, determine whether you need to make some adjustments to your circle. Deep inside, you know what is best for you. Now, rate yourself as a friend. Do you think you are the kind of friend that you desire? If not, what can you change to become the kind of friend that you desire in your life? Be honest. List those things that you can do to improve your friendships.

_____

_____

_____

_____

_____

_____

_____

How To Become An UNSTOPPABLE Black Woman

Dear Black Man:

I love you. I'm not sure who whispered in your ear or convinced you that I was the enemy. I'm not your enemy. You are my king, and I'm your queen. We're royalty. I never wanted our legacy or our beautiful family to be destroyed. I never ever asked to be taken from our country.

At birth, we both received three special gifts: melanin (the substance that gives us the color that everybody else seem to despise, but desires at the same time), and two honorary doctorate degrees in resiliency and creativity. We are a special people. We can do anything, together. We built communities and empires and can do it again (if only we could wake up from this nightmare).

We ended up here, in this place, in this state, and for a few centuries now, it's all we've ever known. Because the Great Creator endowed us with creativity and resiliency, we started anew from where we landed, where we were transplanted. We suffered losses and gains, we rebuilt and overcame, a lot, but we always had an unbreakable bond of love. We lost loved ones, traditions, our language, our culture and our surnames. We started over from scratch and built our family upon new soil. We reluctantly took other people's name. But, we were together, so we rarely complained. That love is now under attack and seems to be unraveling at the speed of light. Our love, our mission, and our vision have become blurred.

For the record, I love every part of you. You were made for me and I was made for you. I love your beautiful body, your intellect, and the way we naturally connect. I love your walk, your swagger, and your style of dress.

Do you know I melt inside when you look at me? I long to look into your beautiful dark eyes and feel your strong hands holding mine. You embrace my body tightly until our heartbeats beat in unison. You reassure me with silence, with your words and many times with your gaze that you would kill for me, lie to save me, or take a bullet and die for me. Now it saddens me that you won't even look my way. On the street, you see me approaching and you turn away while you take the hand of someone else and leave me standing alone. You have a disdain for me that is difficult to comprehend. You no longer think or tell me that my milk chocolate, caramel, mocha, or butter pecan colored skin is beautiful. You no longer think my beautiful thick and strong, natural, curly, hair is suitable. You prefer straight, long hair. You treat me like I'm wrong. I never wanted to perm, weave, or straighten my natural tresses, but I did it because I wanted to be pleasing to your eyes; pleasing to the man I love. Now I'm labeled fake. How can I please you, now? Oh, I wish I knew.

We're made from the same cloth, grew up together in the same village, lived on the same island, arrived here on the same boat, started out on the same team, and learned a new language together in a brand-new environment. We did it! We accomplished so much because of our natural tendencies, creativity, and resiliency. We were lulled to sleep by superficial and calculating people. I'm wide awake, baffled, and can't understand what happened. I see you as I look through the spaces in the Iron Gate; the mental prison that has no boundaries. You look like you are unsure of your position. I can't reach you or speak to you. I can't touch you with my mind or my body. We no longer have each other's back. Somehow, we ended up here—in the middle of the game of life—on opposing teams; at first by force, but now by choice. I don't have the answers. In fact, I have no further questions.

I want you to know that I'm lost without you. If we could trade places for a few seconds, you would understand how much I love and long for you. Some thief intercepted my memo, but I just want you to know……..that I love you, I need you, and I want you! I always have and always will! That will never change, but sadly, everything has changed.

Sincerely,

Your beautiful, proud-to-black, kind and fine, generous, caring, intelligent, attractive, loyal, firm, strong, but submissive, sexy, natural, black woman

P.S. Your sister, girlfriend, wife-to-be, mother, female cousins, grand mammas and all black women who have crossed your path

Chapter Two
Embrace Your Beauty

Sister, you are beautiful and amazing, just the way you are! You have a miraculous, exceptional gift of melanin, that substance that gives you your color. Your skin tone and complexion are envied by many around the world. Have you noticed those who bath in the hot sun, slather on tanning lotions, and visit tanning salons just to turn their skin a darker hue?

Scientists cannot figure out how to extract melanin from black people. Believe me, if they could figure it out, they would have extracted it, studied, concocted a formula, fabricated a liquid or pill, packaged it and have it sitting on shelves this very moment. But they haven't, and you better believe me they are desperately trying to get the formula because they know it holds countless benefits.

Have you taken a good look in the mirror and embraced the fullness of your legs, thighs, and the fullness of your nose? Do you know that people pump lips that *they* once told us were too big? Celebrities and average folks alike spend fortunes on Botox, facelifts, implants, and every kind of injection just to get the full, round buttocks and shapely hips and curves that genetically belong to us.

It's powerful to see a throng of black women embrace their natural beauty, natural hair, and everything about their natural blackness—being confident in their own brown skin.

DON'T BELIEVE THE HYPE

We recognize our natural beauty is coveted and copied by many people. If only some sisters truly accepted their true beauty, in its purest most natural state, they would not buy what the media is selling; trickery, games, deception and the untruths that something is wrong with being black.

The subtle trickery of magazine covers displaying airbrushed images of seemingly flawless people. Movie and TV show casting directors offering bountiful roles to lighter complexioned black women, while making fewer roles available to darker hued women or type casting darker skinned actresses for certain roles, thus disregarding the pure talent and possibly killing the dream of a young black wannabe actress before she auditions for her first role. Inadvertently, young girls and women imitate this "type casting" behavior and try to duplicate physical appearances that are modeled in mainstream media. If some of these girls and women knew the deceit, they'd likely be reluctant to purchase many of the artificial and manmade products (i.e., skin lightening creams, bundles of weaved hair, hair pills and potions to strengthen and lengthen our hair) that line shelves in beauty stores and salons around the world.

Of course, as women, we like to enhance our natural beauty with cosmetics, but a fragment of the black population has been suckered into a game that we are not winning, financially speaking.

Who decides for us what is beautiful? Many images of "black beauty" in magazines, on television, and in movies are of black women with long flowing hair and, in many cases, light skinned complexions. A number of black women are so ashamed of their brown skin that they drain their wallets on whitening agents, bleaching creams and scrubs, and bleaching processes to lighten and whiten their beautiful brown complexion. These black women are determined to lighten their complexion, but don't realize they're compromising their health.

A population of our sisters have allowed someone else to define certain hairstyles as *"real beauty."* Purchasing and wearing hair of any kind, a wig or weave here, and a pair of eye lashes there, for a new look or for cosmetic or medical reasons is one thing. But in the last few decades, *Sisters* have taken the hair game to another level.

Hair is big in Texas (no pun intended), Atlanta, and Baltimore, just to name a few places. Seriously, hair has become a major business and a billion dollar industry, financially disparate for blacks and non-blacks. In fact, financially, the hair industry is a veritable disaster for black people but a monetary goldmine to other races who are cashing in at the bank, everyday.

Consider this...

- If a hairweave cost $770 in Maryland. This includes hair and installation (service) and lasts approximately two months.

- The average tuition at Baltimore City Community College (BCCC) in Baltimore, Maryland is $96 per credit unit/hour (Spring/Summer Semester 2016 for a Maryland resident), or $288 for a standard three credit class

- Using the above information, how many credits or classes could be purchased to send one student to college for one year, with the money ($4,620) that is spent in one year on hair weaves (assuming six hair weave treatments)?

- Answer: _____
  (48 credit hours or 16 classes)

Above example based on hair weave costs, hair weave installation costs and college tuition pricing information obtained online as of October 2015 as shown below.

3 Bundles, Peruvian Double Drawn Bouncy Curl at $185.00 per bundle, would cost $555, at Hair Weave Got It, an online store in Baltimore, Maryland. Hair cost does not include the cost for weave installation. www.hairweavegotit.com

Basic Sew-In Textured Hair costs between $200 and $215 at Hair Weaves & Extensions, a beauty salon in Catonsville, Maryland. Price does not include the cost of the hair installation. www.hairweavesandextensionsmd.com

BCCC Tuition and Fees

Tuition	Winter 2016 Semester	Spring and Summer 2016
Maryland Residents	$88/ credit hour	$96/ credit hour
Out-of-State and Foreign Non Immigrant Residents	$230/ credit hour	$245/ credit hour

Tuition information obtained from Baltimore City Community College www.bccc.edu/tuition

WHAT'S OUR STANDARD FOR BEAUTY?

Who made long, flowing hair the standard or style for black women to follow? Who told us that in order for us to be beautiful, our hair has to be long? Who told us that our natural hair is not good enough? Who do we believe? Why do some of us try to look like everyone else, when we used to be the ones to set the trends for others to follow? Remember Angela Davis and Cicely Tyson and other black women in the 60's and 70's who wore their hair like it grew from their scalps? They defined beauty for black women. Today, we can still define beauty for ourselves. We have the power to set the standard for ourselves.

A few years ago, my husband was traveling in Asia on business. Before returning home, he visited a store in Hong Kong to buy me a gift. The petite, friendly Asian saleswoman asked if he needed help. My husband said he was looking for something special for his wife. The helpful saleswoman recommended an authentic silk robe. Wanting more information, the saleswoman casually asked my husband if his wife had "milky white skin." Needless to say, my husband was shocked and offended a stranger would assume his wife was not black because he is a confident and strong black businessman.

The media continually perpetuate the confident black man and desirable white woman relationship around the world. The perception is that black women are not beautiful enough or worthy of having a black business man. That is a blatant lie.

After my husband recovered from the saleswoman's blatant assumption, he proudly showed her a picture of his beautiful black wife. Sadly, he watched her countenance change. Black women are beautiful and some black men are proud to be married to a black woman (i.e., Will Smith, Denzel Washington, Courtney B. Vance, Grant Hill, Barack Obama, and my husband, just to name a few).

HAIR IS AN ACCESSORY

I'm not anti-hair weaves, perms, or any other hair prop or process that will boost self-esteem, build self-confidence, enhance natural beauty, or afford women the freedom and flexibility to exercise without hair limitations, or help us manage our hair. I've had my share of hair processes and styles from long to short, hot combs, flat irons, rods, perms, plats, twists, braids, and other natural styles. Hair is an accessory that we as black women can use to express ourselves. I just want us to be conscious about why we choose what we choose. Is it because someone else says it's best, or is it because it's best for us individually, personally, professionally, physically, and financially?

At a large shopping mall in Baltimore County, a tall salt-and pepper, caramel brown man possibly on his lunch break graciously approached me. "Hello, Beautiful, it's really nice to see a "*natural*" black woman wearing her natural hair. I hate to see black women with fake hair and long weaves and all that other fake stuff," he said. That was all he said and that was enough. Our exchange was brief, but powerful. He continued on his way, but kept smiling and nodding as he slowly backed away. His message yelled with sincerity, "I don't care what the world is telling you, you are a QUEEN!" For a few seconds, I stepped outside of my mind, sauntered to my throne with my head held high, shoulders back, chest out, feeling confident and comfortable in all of my perfect imperfections and every single one of my flawless flaws. I wasn't looking for validation, but the compliment was a shea butter balm to my spirit.

LOOKING FOR NATURAL BEAUTIES IN MEDIA

I met two black women, Chrissy and Angela, and a black man, Andre, at a funeral repast. As the three of us sat in a packed church dining hall, we had a light-hearted conversation about the image of black women. Andre' posed a simple question to the small group at our table. He said, "Okay ladies, if y'all are convinced that black women don't have image problems, then name me one black woman on TV who does not wear a weave." We all shifted in our chairs, looked at each other as if we were out of lifelines, searching the ceiling for answers, trying to think of somebody, anybody, any woman we could name, so we could shut him up. To our chagrin, we could only name one black woman who didn't wear a hair weave. Angela excitedly shouted, "Robin Roberts!" We all laughed, and Andre' yelled, "SEE! See what I'm saying. Y'all got issues!"

There may be others, but under the pressure of the brother who was winning *that* battle, we couldn't think of any more and had nothing else to say. The man was making a point that black women and girls are trying to look like the images they see in mainstream media. He echoed the sentiments of the brother at the mall. He continued, "See, what y'all sisters don't know is that brothers love to see women wear their natural hair." He also let us in on a man rule and his preference, that a man will flirt with, date, or be intimate with any race of women with any kind of hair, but *he* prefers to be in a relationship with a black woman with natural hair.

I've heard how networks pressure and shun black women because of their hair. I've had countless conversations with friends about celebrities, actresses, newspersons, judges, and ordinary women who've had to conform to get or keep their "good gov'ment jobs" (just kidding). They have to do what they have to do to keep their jobs to pay the bills. But, why do other folks get to make the rules for us.

Tamron Hall is a MSNBC anchor, correspondent for NBC News and NBC's Today Show and a 22-year news and TV journalism veteran. She is also the first African-American woman to co-anchor the NBC Nightly News. She caused a stir when she appeared on the airways last summer (June 2014), wearing her natural hair for the very first time. Many comments were complimentary, but why should a black woman's natural hair be the headline story and the topic of water cooler discussions. As a black professional, why is natural hair an issue?

WHY DID I TORTURE MYSELF?

While at one of my favorite stores, I shifted through the clothing rack and started up a conversation with a 25-year-old gay black male. He shared he used to dress as a woman, but found it too difficult to maintain the look. Shaving facial hair daily, keeping his male member in place when wearing tight-fitting clothes, and wearing ill-fitting heels became too much for him.

As he spoke, I remembered the countless hours I spent in hair salons trying to die, fry, lay, flip, feather, braid, twist and style my hair only to have it sweat back into its' natural curly state within a few days and braided extensions sliding off my hair into the street, one by one (how embarrassing!).

I thought about the artificial nails I wore consecutively for more than 10 years, never taking a break from the acrylic fill-ins, full sets, harsh chemicals and harsh processes that sometimes resulted in a sore nails and on some occasions, a nail fungus. I thought, wow! Now, why did I torture myself like that? Why did I waste so much time and money trying to wear things and styles that were at times painful and oftentimes, painfully expensive to maintain?

The young man I met at the clothing, who was about the same age as my son Bryan, said, "I feel so free now. I wear what I want. I can let my facial hair grow, and I can sport a beard if I want and I dress as a man. The great thing is that I get more male attention now, than I did trying to be something that I wasn't." I smiled at him and I thought to myself, touché' my brother, touché. I wasn't judging him about the male attention comment. I'm happy he embraced who he was and is comfortable embracing his natural (male) self.

When God made black women, he made no mistakes. He made us in every imaginable shade, each one of us totally different from the next, with a unique personality, a specific height, shoe size, body frame and hair texture. Every woman is an irreplaceable creation; a special design in the site of the one who made us. I think it's an insult to God when we don't celebrate ourselves or one another when we are in a purely natural state, without chemicals, potions, implants, or corrective surgeries.

A CULTURE SHOCK TO MY SOUL

In the late 90's, I lived in Westminster, Colorado. The community where I resided was 1% black (at that time). The company where I worked had one black employee, me. The school that my 3rd grader, at the time, attended was 4% black. Living in a small town in Colorado for more than four years was a culture shock to my soul after being born and raised in Baltimore, Maryland, a predominantly black city.

I enjoyed the weather and the picturesque Colorado Rocky Mountains, but was truly disappointed about the lack of interaction among black people. On weekends I visited different cities and became excited when I saw black people, but they were not thrilled to see me. Some would turn their heads when they saw me, but acted as if I were invisible.

This phenomenon could have broken my spirit or made me feel less than the beautiful black woman I am. Even though I'm a friendly person and acknowledge people, no matter their race, I was devastated when black women and men ignored me. I can't understand why that happened so frequently in Denver, and why it continues to happen everyday, no matter what state I visit. Thankfully, after visiting Boulder, Colorado one weekend, my soul was nourished and I made many great lifelong friends.

Throughout our history in this country, we have become conditioned to think that every other race of women, except black women, define beauty. I think many people have fed into the mental images that society has duped us into believing are beautiful. We degrade, criticize, and tease or have been the victim of such mockery by people who have an issue with our blackness, oftentimes by other black people. Sisters, don't be misled, our black is beautiful!

Exercise:

Stop reading for a moment. Go to the nearest full-length mirror, take a good long look at yourself, and write what you see. Examine your natural hair, skin tone, body shape, hands, feet, buttocks, breasts, legs, arms and your facial features. Notice I did not say your size or weight because that can be changed if you want. Write down what you think is wrong with your image (in your opinion only, not what others have said is wrong) and what you see that's right with the image staring back at you? After this exercise is complete, write down three positive words about your image (Ex. "I am attractive", "I love my thick hair", "I think my feet are beautiful", etc.) To embrace your beauty, you must speak positively about yourself. Repeat positive messages about yourself daily.

_____

_____

_____

_____

_____

Tamlyn L. Franklin

Dear God:

I stand here amazed at all that you've created. You existed long before I met you. You knew me before I was formed in my mother's womb. That's amazing! Your depth cannot be touched and your reach has no limits. You are aware of everything, even the secret thoughts of man. You are everywhere. You see everything, but some say they can't see you and don't believe in you. I dare not speak for them, because I see you in the midnight hour, at dawn, and every hour in between. I see you in me. I'm made in your very image.

You have all power. Your great power cannot be denied. You spoke and aligned the planets. At your command, darkness was introduced to light. The sun came forth to light the day and the moon, the night, both shine with all their might. You commanded water to descend, to cover parts of the land, and fill vast oceans, lakes, streams and springs to your exact specifications.

You started mankind with Adam and Eve, now thousands of years later there are billions of human beings. "Reproduce and multiply to replenish the earth" are your commands to every living thing; fowl of the air, insects and animals on land, and creatures in the sea.

Just look at me. The beautiful parts of me that I can see, and all those that I can't see, but I know they are there; heart, brain, liver, lungs, pancreas, bladder, skin, and thick natural hair.

That's why it baffles me when people begin to question their existence. Men are claiming that they were supposed to be women. And women are claiming that they were supposed to be men. How could you create the entire world and get things twisted and confused when it came to them? That makes no sense to me. The creation is perfect, there are no mistakes. You created woman for man, his perfect mate.

You ordained marriage and ordered everything to reproduce and bear fruit after its own kind. You caused the lame to walk, and gave sight to the blind. You are in control. You are God. There is none like you. You are omnipresent, omnipotent, and omniscient. You make grey skies blue.

Everything you created after it was finished, you said it was good. You have a plan for every person, I wish your plan was understood, by everyone. It saddens me to see the number or people who believe blatant and subtle lies, many untruths that are stealing peace and taking lives. I believe in you and can speak for me and no one else. Each person who ever lived must account for her or himself. I choose you dear Lord over everything; you're my provider, my healer, my Master, and my King.

With all my love, heart, mind, body and soul,

Me (Your one-of-a-kind, the only one in all creation, the only me that will ever be)

Chapter Three
Cherish Your Femininity

For the sake of argument, transgender and hermaphrodites are not being addressed here.

Trans what? In today's world, some people are desperately trying to blur the lines between women and men. A few psychologists and other professionals tell people that they are whatever they want to be. They tell whites they can be black and tell a man that they can be a woman, and vice versa, if they choose. I think not! God created man and woman. It was God who created male and female, for his purposes.

While I do not think that women are any less than men, it is a fact that each gender (male and female) has body parts and character traits that the other gender does not possess. Women and females are the ones who bear children and/or produce eggs. Men and males are the ones who produce sperm which fertilize the eggs of a female. No matter how hard a man tries, he will never be able to bear children or produce eggs. Likewise, no matter how much a woman desires to be a man, she will never be able to produce sperm. The characteristics and roles given by the Creator to men and women are distinctly different and should not be confused, misused, or abused.

We know a man is a male human being and a woman is a female human being. *Merriam Webster*[2] defines a gentleman "as a man whose conduct conforms to a high standard of propriety or correct behavior," and a lady is "a woman of refinement." It's clear that a woman and a lady are not one in the same. But, if you desire to improve the image of black women and women in general, don't *act* like a lady, **be** a lady.

It seems more often that women are choosing to defy their roles as women. Some dress like men. They're camouflaging their curves and womanly figures wearing oversized men's clothing and sporting hair in styles making it difficult to determine their gender, avoiding accessories, or cosmetics, giving the appearance of femininity, and seeking to date and *now* legally marry other women, the same women men are competing for.

A WOMAN'S CHANGING ROLE IN TODAY'S WORLD

My son Xavier, who recently finished college, and I were eating breakfast when he confided in me about his struggles at school in South Carolina for the last four years. He shared how difficult it was to date young women on campus because they were only interested in dating other women. That was disheartening to hear. It seems as if the Creator's enemy, Satan, is winning the battle. In talking with people around the country about this issue, learning this is happening at many schools, colleges, in workplaces and communities across the nation.

Women's roles in the home and in the workplace have changed throughout history. Just a few decades ago, women were limited to certain roles such as homemakers, child care workers, secretaries, teachers, and nurses.

Today, women possess many jobs that used to be strictly for men: civil service workers, trash collectors, truck drivers, auto mechanics, medical doctors, architects, engineers, scientists, and so much more. No matter what role a woman assumes, whether she's a stay-at-home mom or not, women have feminine characteristics (menstrual cycle, pregnancy, childbirth, ability to breast feed their babies, menopause, and a fleet of other woman-only traits) that are gender specific that only women can fulfill.

In the 21st century, quite a few men are embodying womanly characteristics. Television programs, music videos, and media are sensationalizing this lifestyle more frequently and making normal male and female relationships and behavior seem abnormal while labeling people who speak out against this as prejudiced and politically incorrect.

From the 1970's to early 1990's, television shows and media, in general, featured feminine black females—no matter their social status. Main black female characters (Florida, Thelma, and Willona) in "Good Times," one of the few black television shows in the 70's, were proud, exuberant, ambitious, morally upright, and most importantly, lady-like.

Another popular television character during the 80s and 90s who epitomized lady-like characteristics was Claire Huxtable on "The Cosby Show." Claire was a lawyer, polite, educated, a decent citizen, an exemplary mother, and a loyal wife. Claire's character and other female characters on that show and others portrayed black women in a positive light.

Fast forward to images of black women in 2015, and we see sitcom characters and reality television personalities portrayed as ruthless, scandalous, married or single who sleep with married men, women who call each other deplorable names, a fighter (physically!), women with little or no morals who'll do anything for the love of money.

People who watch television on a regular basis are being programmed by subtle, and at times, blatant conduct that is stamping and sealing the black woman's persona to the world in a nicely decorated package with indelible images in big bold letters that read: **Black women are loud, combative, angry, aggressive, immoral, ignorant, and undignified.**

Black women, we must not believe, condone, or ratify negative images of us. We must trust and believe in the Creator who made both male and female in his image; the one who created us for his purposes (to replenish the earth). The aforementioned negative stereotype is not lady-like, and I honestly don't believe it is the image of the Creator who is the example of love, patience, kindness, longsuffering, and all things good. Please don't believe the hype that has so many people confused and not accepting their natural role that's been ordained by God. We must refuse to accept what is being delivered to our front steps, in our sacred spaces, and in our most powerful weapon—our minds.

CELEBRATING WOMANHOOD

Women, we are something special and should celebrate womanhood and everything that comes with it. Women are beautiful, nurturing, strong, brilliant, resilient, and great at multi-tasking. Women give life. A woman can carry a baby (one or multiples) in her womb and give birth. A woman can give birth one week and a few days later return to work or to her life-post-pregnancy.

Quite a few of us are so skilled at multi-tasking that we can talk on the phone, whip up a meal, clean and straighten the home in a matter of minutes, check a child's homework, soothe a crying baby, delegate tasks to other members of the household, prepare lunch for the next day, wash a load of clothes, and address our personal needs, not missing a beat and do it all, *after* she gets home from her 9 to 5. Now, tell me that women are not special.

Women are the Creator's masterpiece and should cherish womanhood to the fullest and not run from it like it's a burden. Every woman, no matter her size, shape, or complexion, can be a lady, in all aspects; she can look like one, talk like one, walk like one, dress like one, speak like one and just be one!

Let's take pride in your appearance, from head to toe. Ensure that your hair, nails, legs, hands, feet, and other important parts are well kept. There is absolutely nothing wrong with women having soft skin, smooth legs, and soft hands and feet.

Barbershops, hair salons, nail salons, manicures, pedicures, facials, and razors (for unwanted body hair) are readily available to all. Visit spas or salons as often as necessary to pamper yourself to maintain your appearance. Dress attire should fit your body type and your style of dress. Everyone cannot wear six inch heels or may not feel comfortable in certain clothes, but every woman can find a becoming style that fits her personality.

THE POSSIBILITIES OF CHANGE

I personally know a woman who, for many years, dressed as a man and displayed man-like behavior: she never wore a bra in public even though she was about a size 16 and *needed* a bra for her ample breasts. She sported short hairstyles making it difficult to identify her gender, she spoke loudly, and favored big, baggy clothes hiding her figure; she didn't wear anything that would suggest she was a woman.

Over a period of years, she's made a 180-degree change in her appearance. She never disclosed what made her change. I believe she came to a revelation. She's now a petite size 6, wears stylish, professional attire, favors bras and feminine accessories, and her cute, short pixie hair style gives her a soft demeanor. She honestly doesn't look like the same woman who used to dress and act like a man. She's confident, speaks well, and looks like a woman, acts lady-like and is living as the woman she was created to be. It is possible to change your image.

Women should speak well, at a reasonable volume, and use words that are appropriate, courteous, respectful, uplifting, and positive. Whatever we sow, we reap (in word, in thought, and in our deeds). Women should avoid unattractive behavior such as swearing and cursing like the captain of a ship full of sailors, physically fighting like she's going to win a coveted belt or bounty for the best pugilist, or engaging in any type of behavior that is undignified and unbecoming. Her attitude, words, and language should be appropriate and courteous—not loud, combative, or littered with profanity.

A FIGHT AT THE O.K. K-MART

While sitting in my car on a K-Mart parking lot in Baltimore, Maryland, waiting for my son to come out of the store, I witnessed an argument between two women: a young woman in her 20s and an older woman in her early 50s. As the younger woman walked toward the store, holding the hands of two small children. The older woman drove an SUV headed toward a parking space a little too fast and was being accused of almost hitting the young woman walking with the two small children.

Of course, an argument ensued and so did the cursing and swearing. It was disturbing to watch. Not only were the women treating each other like bitter enemies, but they were behaving badly in front of small children (young black girls) who were in the SUV with the older woman.

The quote, "arguing with a fool proves there are two," immediately came to mind as I witnessed the screaming match. Sometimes, we have to remember that as women, our children will not do what we tell them; they will do what they see us do. We always have a choice in how we respond to situations. Be a lady and walk away.

There are many independent and self-sufficient women who profess that they do not need a man. That is likely very true. I know. I know. A woman can do "bad," all by herself. However, when a woman takes on the man's role and operates in a relationship as if she does not need a man and can do everything for herself, and does not expect or demand that man to do certain things, then that man in her life will not have a problem stepping back and allowing *that* woman to do *her* thing. He may seek out a woman who will allow him to feel "needed" because that is what makes men swell with pride like a tire being pumped with air.

Chivalry is not dead! Many men take great pride in being men (gentlemen) and treating a woman like a lady as such as was so eloquently sung by the Temptations in one of their hit songs, "Treat Her Like a Lady."

Women, allow men to be men:

- If a man takes the time to open doors for you or walk on the outside–while you walk on the inside— closest to the wall, let him.

- When a man stands when you take your seat and holds out your chair or allows you to take his seat if you don't have one, graciously accept his kind gesture.

- When he listens attentively when you speak, goes the extra mile to ensure you are safe and comfortable, talks to you kindly, treats you tenderly and gingerly, genuinely compliments you on a regular basis, showers you with love and affection (publicly and privately), helps you with your sweater or jacket, desires to walk hand in hand, is not afraid to express his deepest emotions, dreams, or fears with you, and treats you with honor and the utmost respect, then relish those moments and thank the Creator for that man!

When you allow men to be men, that gives them pride and the desire to do even more. Men are providers and they enjoy providing safety, shelter, security, sexual healing, and so much more for the women that they truly care about.

When a woman embraces her womanhood and is a lady, a gentleman will recognize her in a crowded room. It won't be anything glaring that will capture his attention- it will be the quiet confidence that oozes from her pores.

While physical appearance is important, confidence is the one ingredient that makes a woman irresistible. Confidence makes a woman sexy (no matter her shape or size). Take care of yourself, and your confidence, your "sexy" will pour out like the finest of wines. What men find sexy is your confidence.

The painter and sculpture from France, Pablo Picasso said, "There are only two types of women – goddesses and doormats." Being a lady does not mean you are going to be perfect or that you desire perfection because that is impossible. But, live in such a way that when people see you, they treat you well because they see a beautiful, confident, unstoppable, lady – a goddess, not a doormat.

Exercise:

Think about the image that you are showing. Think about the language you use, your appearance (your hair, nails, feet, body odor (or lack thereof), clothing, etc.), the way you walk, the way you talk, and your attitude. When people see you, write down how you think *they* would describe you. Now write down what *you* want people to see when they see you. If the two do not match (what others see and what you want others to see when they see you), then describe at least three things that you can do and are willing to adjust today, to make a change. Be honest with yourself. Remember, the goal is to be a lady – a goddess not a doormat.

_____

_____

_____

_____

_____

_____

Hello My Friend:

I recently found a picture of us from way back when. After I dusted the photo, I put it in a frame and placed it on my desk to summon my memory. I want to remember the early years. Things seemed to be so simple back then. I look at our photo and want to go back. I want to go to a place in time when everything was not white and black, at least not in my mind.

We were the tender age of 3 years old, innocent and happy, just as children should be. I was your friend and you were mine, as long as we were together, everything was just fine. I had no idea you were any different from me; we were simply friends. Now that I'm an adult, I see what others could see; two little girls, one white, one black, as different as could be. You had bright blue eyes, straight blond hair and your skin was white as snow.

At the time, I could care less. I honestly didn't know. I had bright brown eyes, two ponytails; hair was dark brown, and my skin color was tan. Obviously, none of that mattered because in the photo we're holding hands. Our smiles are wide and I can see every one of our teeth on full display. Even our eyes are smiling too; looks like we were singing the same tune, and we look as happy as we could be. I love this picture. It's a picture of you and me.

I called my mom to ask her, if she remembered you, she smiled at me through the phone, and told me that you and I stuck together like glue. Her words made my heart smile. I hope you have a copy of our photo somewhere in your life files.

After age four, we saw each other no more. There was a shift. It was only a matter of time before I became aware of our differences. I wonder if you became aware at the same time. I was devastated to learn of the evil. It was difficult for my young mind to comprehend. It was worse than learning there was no Santa. I didn't want that fantasy to end.

DISCOVERING BEING BLACK

I didn't know having brown skin was perceived as something bad until we moved (I was around age 6). My parents decided we needed to move after the black people in our neighborhood were being inundated with free drugs (from Lord knows who?). Someone had a plan, but my parents were wise and sought out a safe place, but we were all in for a surprise. When we moved to a new neighborhood, where there were no blacks save one, everyone there seemed angry and scared.

I wondered why people were afraid. We were no different from them, only the color of our hair and eyes, and the color of our skin. Okay. So what? Their skin was white and my skin was brown, did that make it right for them to throw me to the ground, or hurl rocks and sticks at our home or chase me and my brother home from school, or spray paint our car, or poison our dog with tainted food?

I could go on and on, but you get the point. I just didn't (and still don't) understand the rage and all the hate. We were peaceful people who we were just trying to live. We weren't causing any trouble. *We* should have been scared and angry. It was the other neighborhood kids who had behavior beyond bad, it was evil. I wonder why they were so violent and cruel, were they following someone else's lead, or were they just being kids, doing mischievous things? I wonder.

At a very young age, my siblings and I learned firsthand about deep-seated hate. I wonder if you had similar experiences. I wonder if you can relate. Around age 10, I began to understand more about civil rights, but I couldn't understand, to save my life, why basic civil rights were such a fight. Why was skin color such a big deal? Didn't all people bleed red blood? Weren't we all created by the same God? I couldn't understand why dogs were used to attack or why fire hoses were turned on people that were black, or why crosses were burned on our front lawn, and why our white neighbors were so mean and carried all kinds of weapons, and why they wore white sheets at night (sometimes marched during the day), those were very scary times. My friend, could you make sense of those things? Could you make sense of those times?

I fast forward a few decades and I face forward in a new century and notice many things. There is goodness everywhere. Sadly, other things have not changed and that is a downright shame. Homes of black people are still being burned to the ground, destroyed with spray paint, derogatory hateful words colored on the walls, and many other heinous things, simply unthinkable things, someone was found hung from a tree (but it was reported that it was he himself that did that thing).

LIVING WHILE BLACK

Black folks are being profiled daily, mostly for driving while black, incarcerated for minor offenses and killed for no reason at all. In New Jersey, a black man was recently killed for selling loose cigarettes. In Florida, a young black boy was killed for carrying in his hands a cell phone, a soft drink and candy. Why are those two souls no more? Why do blacks seem to be under attack? Why are countless black people gone, killed on the streets, in broad daylight, in jail cells, in patrol cars, in police wagons, and some in their own homes? Black men (now women) seem to be the targeted, for being black, but when they are stopped and arrested or killed, the police reports read something else. The court system was designed by whites, so I guess it should be no surprise.

Events of the past that are still on file in my mind and every time we turn around, there is yet another painful reminder. Being black in the world is different from being white. Being black in this world means there is a constant fight; not just for civil, but for basic human rights. There are so many concerns for blacks throughout the land, on our jobs, in the home of every black woman and man.

I have a beautiful family, and we are unapologetically black. We have souls, and we love hard, tell me, what's wrong with that! We live in world that has been colored black and white. We seem to always end up on the wrong side of right. I'm a bit uneasy each time one of our birds leaves the nest, I try to keep my mind from thinking if they will be stopped while flying, or if they take a different route, will someone tail them, or cage them, or do something worse.

I thought of calling for help recently when my husband, a 6 foot black man, while walking for exercise, seemed to be in distress and in need of medical attention, but decided against making the call because of the climate and the ostensible racial tension. How sad is this? To live in a climate, a city, a country, a world where, you must think ahead, if you are black and you call for help, you may just end up dead. This is my reality. This is our reality.

Some neighborhoods and cities (even some states), that are predominantly white, are still "off limits" to blacks. We notice the looks from some people. Their mouths are closed, but their eyes shout, "You are not welcome here, get out!" We may be black, but we work for what we have, we can buy what we please. Isn't all money green?" I guess it's naïve to think that money would make the world blind to color.

I wonder what life was like for you growing up in the same world that I speak of. I wonder if you have siblings or had children? I wonder if you are the same little girl; on the inside, the only side that really matters. I wonder where you went after nursery school; if you attended public or private school. I wonder if you had new books and modern classrooms or did you have tattered books, in failing schools, but still had a love for learning, like me? I wonder where you moved, if you lived in harmony and peace, or if you were chased home from school, or if you had to dodge rocks and sticks.

I wonder when you became an adult, if you are still alive, if you ever married and did you go to college? I can't believe how quickly life has flown by; it's been over 40 years. Hopefully we can meet again someday, my best childhood friend. But, if we don't, I will always remember the good years, when life was so simple; back then.

Big hug and lots of love,

Your childhood friend (from back then, as a child, when things used to be so simple)

Chapter Four
FORGIVE TO BE FORGIVEN

But, I didn't cause this mess! I don't know why "I" have to apologize. I wish I would say I'm sorry to him/her or beg his/her forgiveness for something I didn't start, but I know how to end it. Have you ever felt like this? Do you ever feel like God is just not hearing your cries for whatever you have prayed and begged for? Have you uttered a prayer only to have the answer come back: "Not right now—in due time," or "No"?

Oftentimes we pray expecting every answer to be yes and every promise to be delivered when we think it should be delivered. Sometimes we reject God, resist the Spirit, or blatantly disobey because we want what we want, and we want to satisfy ourselves—no matter what.

SURRENDER TO FORGIVE

I recently realized I had been praying for more than a decade that I would genuinely learn how to forgive others and the prayer had been answered, finally.

Actually, my prayer has been answered because "I" finally surrendered. It has taken me many years (I mean yeeearrrrzz) to let go of my position and *my* **RIGHT to be MAD AS HELL!**

A Friday morning as I walked around the track (striving for my 10,000 steps, it's a challenge, but I must do it for my wealth— my health is my wealth), the Spirit told me to break down a barrier that I've had with a family member. I didn't realize there was a barrier. I certainly didn't feel like *I* had built a barrier. But thank God for the Spirit that reveals to us, when we are ready to receive, what we need to do to see our flaws and / or correct *our* behavior.

The Spirit told *me* that I needed to be the bigger person and told *me* to apologize for anything that I've said or done in our relationship that may have caused hurt or pain to that person and ask them for their forgiveness. Initially, I resisted. *There is no way I'm doing that*, I thought. I couldn't believe that the Spirit was telling me to do something so difficult; ask them for their forgiveness! (You mean I have to let go of my pride). But, I kept walking and praying. Every lap around the track, I kept thinking this was not the answer I was waiting for. I began to slowly ease off of my position. As I continued walking, I started gradually accepting what the Spirit was telling me. At first, I thought, "You want me to do what?" My pride and my position that I've had for more than a decade (that I'm right and I didn't do anything wrong to cause this MESS in the first place) kept me from surrendering. But, I know that I couldn't have done it one day sooner, because I just was not ready to let go of my anger.

I listened to the Spirit and did my best to respond to my specific instructions. Thank God for grace and mercy! Before I talked myself out of doing what was right (for me at this time) and before busying myself with anything else, I sent a text message to the family member. I didn't feel comfortable doing it face to face (Jesus knows my every weakness), but knew I had to listen to the Spirit and not quench it (I was afraid of the consequences of *me* not listening).

For a split second, I felt sad that I had been so stubborn and blind to the truth and for the fact that I would look at myself every day in my full length mirror, but could not see myself completely. I should have been praying to Jesus, "Jesus, please help me to see me and to see more of you in me, every day. Amen." Then, almost immediately after I hit send, and my text was delivered, I felt an unspeakable joy! I felt like a backpack packed full of bricks (don't need any more bricks - thank you Jesus!) had been lifted off of my back and shoulders. I almost ran my final lap, but decided not to overdo it. (I had already walked 5 miles!)

After listening to and responding to the guidance of the Holy Spirit, the family member, later that day, apologized to me for any pain they may have caused me. Jesus will fix it after a while. See, I had been holding on to my anger for so long, I didn't realize that I was meticulously and silently building a wall like a skilled brick layer. I didn't realize that the wall between us had become so thick and solid that not even a bulldozer could knock it down.

Every time I rehearsed, reviewed or relived my pain, I would add a brick, then they would add a brick, then I would add another brick or a few boulders, and the cycle of wall-building continued until each encounter or even the very thought of one another would cause a physical reaction (headaches, migraines, seething anger where we couldn't even see, digestive problems, hair loss, feeling mentally stuck, etc.) in one or both of us.

Since that moment at the track, the self-inflicted burdens of anger, hostility, frustration, and everything else that is unhealthy, have been lifted. See, no one could see what I was feeling on the inside. As a human being and especially as a woman, I am good at hiding my sinful nature. No one knows our true heart and all of our sinful behavior or our sinful nature except God. People only know about the sins we confess or what they discover (women are genius at covering up stuff). Others never know what we have in our hearts. Sometimes, we don't even understand it ourselves. But it's usually *me* that keeps me stuck, for whatever reason—pride, stubbornness, embarrassment, shame, disappointment, etc.

I just want to say that I feel lighter! I'm at peace. Our entire house feels like a massive stopper has been removed to let out the cesspool of hurt that was not only drowning me and the other person, but everyone connected to us. Now we can all breathe with ease the sweet fragrance of forgiveness and live in peace. I believe that when we do our best (follow the Holy Spirit's guidance and let go of our position to be right or our right to be angry, or our right and privilege to be mad because of what someone else has done to us or not done for us), then God will do the rest!

FORGIVENESS REQUIRES STRENGTH

Forgiveness requires courage. Mahatma Gandhi said, "The weak can never forgive. Forgiveness is the attribute of the strong." It takes courage to say I'm sorry and it takes even more courage to say I forgive you when you've been the recipient of someone's dispensed offenses. It may be especially difficult if you were the victim of circumstance. It takes courage to be the bigger person, to open the lines of communication, to break the ice, to begin to heal a broken or severed relationship. God is able to help.

Sometimes *we* need forgiveness for things that we may have said or done that may have caused someone else pain. Other times we may need to forgive someone who has done something egregious to us.

Wherever we happen to be today with respect to forgiveness, we must be mindful of God's principle regarding forgives. In the book of Matthew 16:5, the word clearly states: But if you do not **forgive** others their sins, your Father will not **forgive** your sins. Enough said.

Every person has been on either side of the forgiveness coin because no one is perfect. We all make mistakes and have mess-ups from time to time. We may say something foolish that we wish we could erase from the record and at times do things that we desperately wish we could undo.

We knowingly and sometimes unknowingly cause irreparable damage, pain, and discomfort to others with careless comments, harsh words, sharp tongues, or many other kinds of offensive behavior. We have to forgive in order to be forgiven. The way we forgive, is the way we will be forgiven.

I love the anonymous quote, "To forgive is to set a prisoner free and discover that the prisoner was you." This quote hit me like the bag of bricks that I used to carry like a disciplined soldier.

For years, I held on to unforgiveness and kept it close to me—like it was a dear friend. I wore my hurt like a badge of honor. I can assure you that once I relinquished control of my anger, pride, and my position, I not only freed the prisoner that I held captive for so long, but also learned that the prisoner had been me all along.

FIND HEALING THROUGH FORGIVENESS

Forgiveness frees your mind, heals your body, lifts your spirits, and helps you to get "unstuck." Forgiveness is the beginning of healing. One of my favorite books is *You Can Heal Your Life* by Louise L. Hay. This book provides tips for healing one's life and a helpful list that correlates physical problems with probable mental causes. Dr. Hay offers affirmations or new thought processes to overcome or alleviate physical problems to help you get to the root of diseases. Hay says that every disease (dis-ease) is a result of some unforgiveness (of oneself or others).

In the past few months, I began to suffer from what I diagnosed as acid reflux. I awakened each morning with indigestion, constant burping before I ate a single bite of food. I got severe heartburn and felt full with only a few small bites of food. I'd say, "This must be acid reflux." Then, I'd call my mom and she'd say, "Yes, what you've described sounds like acid reflux. Get you some Tums."

Before making an appointment to see my doctor or purchasing some over the counter medication, I'd resort to my book. Whatever I was experiencing physically, I'd flip to the index to see if the problem was listed. I'd usually discover the probable causes for many common ailments:

Problem	Probable cause	New thought pattern
Lower back	Fear of money. Lack of financial support	I trust the process of life.
Boils	Anger. Boiled over. Seething.	I express love. I am at peace.
Heartburn	Fear. Fear. Fear	I trust the process of life.
Indigestion	Gut-level fear, dread, anxiety.	I digest all new experiences.

The truth of the matter is that after I opened my heart and mind to forgiveness, as I described earlier, the symptoms gradually desisted without medication or medical intervention. I'm a believer that if we truly desire to be released from mental bondage and get "unstuck", then we need to begin with forgiveness. Forgiveness will give us room to move forward as we walk in our purpose.

Exercise:

Examine your life, your health, and your progress. Do you ever feel stuck? <u>Do you need to be forgiven?</u> If yes, write down who or what you need forgiveness from and genuinely change or ask for forgiveness so you can begin to heal your life. Forgiveness will allow you to move on.

_____

_____

_____

_____

_____

_____

_____

_____

<u>Do you have someone of something to forgive?</u> Fill in the blanks with your honest answers. If the person that you need to forgive is you, don't hesitate to forgive yourself. If the person you need to forgive is no longer living, you can still forgive them so you can begin to heal.

I forgive _____ (person) for _____ (offense).

I forgive _____ (person) for _____ (offense).

I forgive _____ (person) for _____ (offense).

I forgive _____ (person) for _____ (offense).

I forgive _____ (person) for _____ (offense).

I forgive _____ (person) for _____ (offense).

I forgive _____ (person) for _____ (offense).

Forgiving is not forgetting. Forgiving is letting go of the hurt.

Dear Ancestors:

As I stand on your broad, powerful shoulders and look back at the road that leads to the past, your past, our past, I marvel at your strength. The road is quite narrow and stretches for miles; miles that outnumber my existence. Trees line the road like soldiers standing at attention. Some of the trees are silent. Some are still. They are trying to forget the deeds that were done, on their watch, with their help. They were accessories to crimes against innocent people whose greatest crime was the color of skin.

I can see their sadness that extends from their verdant tops which kiss the sky, to their extensive roots that are deeply and tightly ingrained in the earth, like long braided hair. Their mighty branches were required, against their will, to hold human bodies, old and young bodies, as they hung, suffered, slowly and painfully died, against their will, for simply being black, at such a time. They witnessed the wicked at work; spewing ample venom, cheering for the death angel, rejoicing in suffering of a people, and watching forlorn black folks mourn their great losses.

Like you, they wish they could erase those memories that disturb their peace. The trees remember. We remember. They are still standing and so are we.

The tree-lined road is sitting still and quiet, now that the dust has settled, my mistake; it only appears to have settled. There is no one in sight but, I hear a slight sound.

I listen carefully to the silence that was once very loud in my inner ear. I slowly stroll in the direction of the faint noise, toward a road where derelict shacks once stood. I begin to hear whimpers. The whimpering is becoming loud and the cries are changing to screams. I'm turning in circles with my hands covering my ears trying to muffle the sound, but I can't. I can't drown out the pain that I can now see with my naked eyes—small children being snatched from their mommas, and husbands being separated from wives.

I watch you begging to be released, from the reality of your captivity. Crying and asking, "Who authorized this brutal and horrific trade, me and my family, my people displayed on the auction block, being sold as slaves? How can you own me, own us, when we were born FREE? How can you hold me captive or sell me for a fee, to the highest bidder? God! Is this real? Please HELP ME!"

I see heavy leather whips hanging from wooden fences, both still glistening with your blood; blood that remains on the hands of every wicked person who benefited from your labor, free labor, slave labor -- an enterprise that had devastating effects on people who made valiant efforts to flee. The effects are everlasting, even the blind can see. When you attempted to flee they called you runaways. RUNAWAYS! They posted signs on trees; for your safe return, rewards they would gladly pay. Did they think you wanted to stay, work for no pay, and stay with the enemy, stay away from your loved ones, and never reunite with your families to whom you were deeply and emotionally connected, and now detached in every way? No way! You would run away again, and again, even if you had no place to stay. Who could blame you? Could they?

The stories are coming at me so fast that I'm desperately trying to hear them all. You mean they raped you, and would take you whenever then felt the urge. They threw you scraps of food scarcely fit for an animal to eat. They gave you corn and salty meat, very little fruits and vegetables, but plenty of animal feet to eat. They let you and your family sleep in a small shack, you and yours in the cramped attic, you and yours in a tiny cell with no windows, a dirt floor and cement walls. They worked you from sunrise to well into the night. They promised to pay you and give you your freedom papers, but the time was never right. They worked you in their yards, you in their kitchens and salons. They made you a barber, you a butler, you a maid, and you a farmer. They made you a chauffeur. Oh, the nerve! They branded you. They renamed you. They dared you to leave. Let me get this right? They begged you to stay. They favored you over others. They kept you in chains. They put shackles on your feet. They hung your father from a tree. How could this be?

Like roaring lions, they have always been on the prowl, walking about, seeking whom and what they could devour. They captured us in our country where we were born happy and free. They enslaved us and reaped lifelong benefits of everything we made. They seem to have always had the upper hand. They "discovered" land and took what they pleased, then divided the rest between other thieves, from distant places. They accumulated much of their wealth from free slave labor. They exhibited the most heinous, criminal, and terrorist-like acts and behavior. Still to this day, they have never disseminated any to us, from whom their wealth was generated. They own much land and have great assets for themselves and generations (their kin folk) to come. What recompense did we get for our stolen years? We received much torture and pain and we were played for nothing but fools. We were promised some land, forty acres and a mule. The promises were empty, like a cup with a hole, a cup that cannot be filled. Will they ever pay for the crimes that were done? Where is the justice that never found us? Should we just forget?

For all you've been through, you have my utmost respect. I'm thankful that you had the strength to endure what may have bruised my body, broken my spirit, or killed me or my will to give life to future generations, if I had been born at such a time. It angers me so much to hear of the horrific acts against us, it makes my heart ache and brings me to tears. How did you muster the strength to get through those tumultuous times, the uncertain days, and the rough years? How did you endure being cheated, beaten, and severely mistreated? How did you overcome being abated and hated, isolated and incarcerated, mutilated and violated, manipulated and miseducated, emasculated and devaluated, repudiated and evaluated, castrated and desecrated, and estranged from your own country? Help me to understand the essence of you. Help me to understand your strength. I hope to hear from you.

Humbly and respectfully,

Your descendant

Dear Descendant:

Allow me to make sense of the past, so you can appreciate the present, and walk boldly into the future. When you look into my past, you see insurmountable pain. Never forget. But, remember to count your blessings. The source of my strength comes from the Creator and his holy word. Understand the power of the word–it can cut, crush, soothe, heal, and create.

My soul looks back too and wonders how I made it through the fire. It was difficult and seemed unfair. I dare not forget to mention the kind folks who helped us along the way. They put themselves in danger, helped us escape and hide, they gave us what we may have needed, they were really angels in disguise. May they be blessed, evermore.

Whenever I become discouraged, I read Psalm 37, written by David. Every line ministers to me. I want you to know its' power to soothe and heal your spirit and calm your rage and ire.

¹ Don't worry about the wicked
  or envy those who do wrong.
² For like grass, they soon fade away.
  Like spring flowers, they soon wither.

³ Trust in the LORD and do good.
  Then you will live safely in the land and prosper.
⁴ Take delight in the LORD,
  and he will give you your heart's desires.

⁵ Commit everything you do to the LORD.
  Trust him, and he will help you.
⁶ He will make your innocence radiate like the dawn,
  and the justice of your cause will shine like the noonday sun.

⁷ Be still in the presence of the LORD,
  and wait patiently for him to act.
  Don't worry about evil people who prosper
  or fret about their wicked schemes.

⁸ Stop being angry!
  Turn from your rage!
  Do not lose your temper—
  it only leads to harm.
⁹ For the wicked will be destroyed,
  but those who trust in the LORD will possess the land.

¹⁰ Soon the wicked will disappear.
  Though you look for them, they will be gone.
¹¹ The lowly will possess the land
  and will live in peace and prosperity.

¹² The wicked plot against the godly;
  they snarl at them in defiance.
¹³ But the Lord just laughs,
  for he sees their day of judgment coming.

¹⁴ The wicked draw their swords
  and string their bows
  to kill the poor and the oppressed,
  to slaughter those who do right.
¹⁵ But their swords will stab their own hearts,
  and their bows will be broken.

¹⁶ It is better to be godly and have little
  than to be evil and rich.
¹⁷ For the strength of the wicked will be shattered,
  but the Lord takes care of the godly.

¹⁸ Day by day the Lord takes care of the innocent,
  and they will receive an inheritance that lasts forever.
¹⁹ They will not be disgraced in hard times;
  even in famine they will have more than enough.

20 But the wicked will die.
  The Lord's enemies are like flowers in a field—
  they will disappear like smoke.

21 The wicked borrow and never repay,
  but the godly are generous givers.
22 Those the Lord blesses will possess the land,
  but those he curses will die.

23 The Lord directs the steps of the godly.
  He delights in every detail of their lives.
24 Though they stumble, they will never fall,
  for the Lord holds them by the hand.

25 Once I was young, and now I am old.
  Yet I have never seen the godly abandoned
  or their children begging for bread.
26 The godly always give generous loans to others,
  and their children are a blessing.

27 Turn from evil and do good,
  and you will live in the land forever.
28 For the Lord loves justice,
  and he will never abandon the godly.

  He will keep them safe forever,
  but the children of the wicked will die.

29 The godly will possess the land
   and will live there forever.

30 The godly offer good counsel;
   they teach right from wrong.
31 They have made God's law their own,
   so they will never slip from his path.

32 The wicked wait in ambush for the godly,
   looking for an excuse to kill them.
33 But the LORD will not let the wicked succeed
   or let the godly be condemned when they are put on trial.

34 Put your hope in the LORD.
   Travel steadily along his path.
   He will honor you by giving you the land.
   You will see the wicked destroyed.

35 I have seen wicked and ruthless people
   flourishing like a tree in its native soil.
36 But when I looked again, they were gone!
   Though I searched for them, I could not find them!

37 Look at those who are honest and good,
   for a wonderful future awaits those who love peace.
38 But the rebellious will be destroyed;
   they have no future.

³⁹ The LORD rescues the godly;
   he is their fortress in times of trouble.
⁴⁰ The LORD helps them,
   rescuing them from the wicked.
   He saves them,
   and they find shelter in him.

Thank you for coming to me. Thank you for remembering me. Every time you make time and take time to be still and quiet, that gives me a chance to whisper to you, to speak to you, to direct you. Did you know that, "Silence brings wisdom of the ancestors" and "Dreams are voices of ancestors"? God speaks to us through his word and I speak to you through proverbs. I leave you with these, I hope you take heed. These lessons are for your learning and serve as a blueprint for freedom.

AFRICAN & OTHER PROVERBS:

- "Every day of your life is a page of your history." ~Arabian Proverb

- "He who forgives ends the quarrel." ~unknown

- "A fight between grasshoppers is a joy to the crow." ~ Lesotho Proverb

- "A society grows great when old men plant trees whose shade they know they shall never sit in." ~ Greek Proverb

- "A wise person will always find a way." ~ Tanzanian proverb

- "One who loves you, warns you." ~ Uganda Proverb

- "By the time the fool has learned the game, the players have dispersed." ~ Ashanti Proverb.

- "Children are the reward of life." ~ African proverb.

- "Don't set sail using someone else's star." (Avoid copying someone else. Just because someone has been successful in what he/she does should not be what will make you do the same thing and expect to be successful.) ~ African proverb

- "Dreams are voices of ancestors." ~ African proverb

- "God knows the things of tomorrow." – Burundi

- "He that digs up a grave for his enemy may be digging it for himself."

- "He who fears the sun will not become chief." ~ Kenyan proverb

- "He who learns teaches." ~ Ethiopian proverb

- "He who trusts in God lacks nothing." ~ Swahili

- "If relatives help each other, what evil can hurt them?" ~ unknown

- "If there is character, ugliness becomes beauty; if there is none, beauty becomes ugliness." ~ Nigerian proverb

- "If you close your eyes because of the bad people around you, you will not see the good people passing by." ~ unknown

- "If you don't know where you are going, any road will take you there." ~Uganda

- "If you want to go quickly, go alone. If you want to go far, go together." ~ African proverb

- "In the moment of crisis, the wise build bridges and the foolish build dams." ~ Nigerian proverb

- "It is not what you are called, but what you answer to." ~ African Proverb

- "Love put the eaglet out of its nest." ~ Kenyan proverb

- "Make some money, but don't let money make you." ~ Tanzania

- "Patience is the key which solves all problems." ~ Sudanese

- "The heart of a wise man lies quiet like limpid water." ~ Cameroon proverb

- "The soul would have no rainbow if the eyes didn't have tears."

- "There is no medicine to cure hatred."

- "To be able to love other people you must be able to love yourself." ~African Proverb

- "To be without friends is to be poor indeed." ~ Tanzanian Proverb

- "Unity is strength, division is weakness." ~ Swahili proverb

- "Wealth, if you use it, comes to an end; learning, if you use it, increases." ~Swahili Proverb

- "What you give you get, ten times over." ~ Yoruba proverb

- "What you help a child to love can be more important than what you help him to learn." ~African Proverb

- "When you know who his friend is, you know who he is." ~ unknown

- "Whenever a man wakes up become his morning." (all hope is not lost or it's never too late to kick start your life) ~ African proverb

- "Where a woman rules, streams run uphill." *(Women can make wonderful things happen.)* ~ Ethiopian proverb

- "Wisdom does not come overnight." ~ Somali proverb

- "You should not sleep outside just because someone else did it and was lucky." ~ Tonga proverb.

- "Do not look where you fell, but where you slipped." (Don't look at your mistakes; look at what caused you to make the mistakes otherwise you may repeat the mistake.) ~ African proverb

- "When you are rich, you are hated; when you are poor, you are despised."

- "He who is destined for power does not have to fight for it."

- "A close friend can become a close enemy."

- "If a child washes his hands he could eat with kings." (If you prepare and allow yourself to be well-trained, when you have the opportunity, you will achieve a lot and be favored in due course.)

- "A roaring lion kills no game." (You cannot achieve or gain anything by mere sitting around and just talking about it).

- "If you offend, ask for a pardon; if offended forgive." *(what goes around, comes around)*

- "The fool speaks, the wise man listens." ~ Ethiopian proverb

- "When the rain falls on the leopard it wets the spots on his skin but does not wash them off." *(A person's nature is not changed by circumstances.)* ~ unknown

- "Strong people make things happen; weak people let things happen." ~unknown

- "Smooth seas do not make skillful sailors." ~ African Proverb

PERSONAL FAVORITES

- "You must act as if it is impossible to fail." ~ Ashanti proverb

- "When there is no enemy within, the enemies outside cannot hurt you." ~ unknown

- "Kindness is a language which the blind can see, and the deaf can hear." ~ African Proverb

- "More precious than our children are the children of our children." ~ Egyptian Proverb

- "However long the night, the dawn will break." (*No situation is permanent. There is hope for tomorrow*). ~ African proverb

ALL TIME FAVORITE

- "Traveling is learning." – Kenyan Proverb

What will keep you moving forward when every effort is made to annihilate, obliterate, and exterminate your very existence? The things that will sustain you, my child, are the things that have been ingrained in you, everything that has been passed on to you and everything that comprises you; your strength, resilience, courage, creativity, melanin, perseverance, and wisdom. Keep them safe.

God equipped you to be born at such a time. That is the reason why you continue to rise. Repeat after me…And Still I Rise!

Love forever,

Your Ancestor ("I come as one, but I stand as 10,000.")

Chapter Five
NEVER GIVE UP

I'm what? Excuse me? Did you say pregnant? *Dear God, I know she didn't just say that I'm pregnant!* But, Doc, I just received my college acceptance letter to go to engineering school in Pennsylvania. I always wanted to go to college out of state. *Oh God! What am I going to do? I'm pregnant. What is mommy going to say? Sweet Jesus! What is dad going to say? Breathe.* I sigh deeply. I swallow hard. The air lodged in my throat seems to be the size of a golf ball. What are my two brothers going to say? What is my sister going to think? *I'm pregnant.* What is my grandmother going to say? *Jesus!* What is my great grandfather going to say? *Oh Lawd (please help me)! I can't breathe. Help me Jesus!* How can I have a baby and go to college away from home? Come on Tam? Think! You got to do something! Everyone was so happy to hear that I was going away to college to become an engineer. They will all be so disappointed in me. *Help me God. I can't be pregnant. You wouldn't do this? Would you God?*

[God was probably looking down on me saying," Excuse you. You are the one who lay down and got pregnant, missy."]

I mean, you know the plan, right God? The plan is for me to go to college in Pennsylvania, live on campus, get the full college experience, graduate with a degree in engineering, get a job, get married, then have children, and live happily ever after, in that order. Not!

Now what am I going to do? I'm pregnant and I'm not married. OH GOD!!!!!! What is everyone going to say? I can hear people gossiping and whispering now, "You know she isn't even married. Look at her. She's pregnant. Unh, unh, unh!"

Never give up. When plan A is not working, gather your thoughts, pick up from where you are and go to plan B. If plan B does not work, then you must move on to plan C. There are 26 letters in the alphabet. You must keep pushing and moving forward even if planning causes you to exhaust all 26 letters. There is always something you can do. The smallest change or effort can produce the greatest results. You will never know if you do not keep going.

When I learned that I was pregnant, shortly after my 19th birthday, I was initially disappointed in myself. I had a plan for my life and thought that the pregnancy meant that my plan would be voided. Deep down inside, I knew that I could not quit. I had to use my mind and consider what I could do to continue toward my goal. Not having the baby was never considered. My greatest concern was how to move forward with the baby. Going to college was not optional. I was going to college and I was going to become an electrical engineer, even though I wasn't even sure at the time what being an engineer truly meant.

TELLING MY MOM

I picked up the phone and called my mother. She was at work and answered the phone on the first ring. When I heard her voice I started shaking like I had just finished drinking a gallon of coffee. I said, "Mom, I need to talk to you." After that statement, nothing came out of my mouth except loud pitiful noises. I broke down. I burst out crying. I was crying uncontrollably.

My mom was at work at the time and was probably scared out of her mind once she heard my cries. She just kept asking trying not to yell, "What's wrong, what's wrong Tammy, what's wrong?" I could hear the panic through the telephone. She could feel my distress through the telephone. I tried to tell her, but the words wouldn't budge. I was so afraid that I was going to disappoint her with my news. Without any warning, I just hung up the phone. I just couldn't speak. I stood there looking at the phone for a few minutes, just balling.

My mom must have left work immediately after she heard the dial tone, jumped in her car, and sped all the way home, because not long after I hung up, it seemed like only minutes before she was standing in my bedroom looking at me with fear in her eyes.

When I looked up and saw the distress on her face and the sincere concern in her eyes, I just blurted out, "I'm pregnant."

She held her chest and tried to put her heart back in place and looked at me and said, "Is that all?" She gently patted her heart again, smiled and exhaled a big sigh of relief. She said, "Girl, I thought you had killed somebody." I wiped my tears, smiled and I sighed. *[My mom is so funny. Killed somebody! Jesus mom!]* I could breathe again. She grabbed me, hugged me, and assured me that everything would be alright. She told me that I would be able to reach every goal I had set for myself. She told me that I wasn't the first woman to be pregnant with a plan. I had to work my plan being pregnant or revise my plan. She told me that I wouldn't be the last woman to have to walk in those shoes. She told me not to worry about what anyone had to say. She said don't worry about family members, siblings, daddy, friends, or anybody else. She told me not to listen to naysayers. I listened to her.

I was so thankful that I had the support of my mom. She provided the encouragement that I needed to come up with plan B. Sometimes we just need to talk with someone to give us time to gather our thoughts and come up with ways to move forward. When we fall down, we must get up and try again or try something new. If a baby falls, when learning to walk, he doesn't just sit there; he will get up and try again, and again, and again. Likewise, when plan A is not working for us, we have the same choice that the baby has. We can sit there and accept the fact that we cannot walk or we can get up and try again (that's plan B). If we fall again, we get back up and try again (that's' plan C).

THE COURAGE TO SUCCEED—NO MATTER WHAT

Being pregnant is not a death sentence. Having any kind of disorder or disease is not a death sentence. Nor is any other thing that one could potentially encounter. There may be challenges and events in our lives that seem insurmountable, but we have the ability to overcome anything. We have the power to overcome any challenge that may come our way. As long as we have breath in our bodies, a mind to think, and the will to succeed, then we can overcome.

A couple of years ago, my sister Gwen and I went to Oprah's Life Class in Houston. (Going to the Oprah Show was on my vision board!) One of the guests on the show was a young man with no arms and no legs. He was literally a head with a two-foot torso. After using the strength in his body, he managed to get out of his seat in the audience and get up on the stage.

Watching him move and maneuver his body was something to behold. He spoke into the microphone that was secured to his shirt and shared his story about wanting to give up as a child because he had a limited scope. He didn't believe that he could achieve what normal children could achieve because of his lack of extremities. He said at a young age he talked with his parents and was encouraged to dream big. In his teenage years he changed his belief and after he changed his mind, he changed his life. He overcame his limited beliefs and decided that everything that he wanted, he was going to achieve. He participated in sports, traveled extensively, and even found a beautiful woman whom he married. Getting married was one of his biggest dreams. He achieved great things with no arms and no legs. He was successful because he did not quit on himself, he didn't quit on life, he didn't quit on achieving his goals and dreams.

After I learned that I was pregnant, I knew that going out of state was not prudent, so I decided to go to the local University, MSU (HBCU). Yeah Morgan! I picked up an application, enrolled, was accepted, started school (pregnant from day 1), and continued straight through until the Friday before spring break. I only missed one day of college. It was the day before the start of spring break. That was the day my water broke, the day my son was born, the Friday before spring break, on a beautiful sunny day, in March of 1988.

After spring break, the challenge became real. There were many days I didn't get a break; my baby was in need of my attention or I had an assignment to complete. I stayed up all night on many occasions, but still had to go to work, with zero hours of sleep. I wanted to quit almost every semester and sometimes as often as every week. It was no easy feat by a long shot.

I took 15 to 17 credits every semester while caring for an infant, as I studied and worked on the weekends five years straight. I took 3 to 6 credits every summer, completed lab assignments and soothed my baby when he was teething. I may have missed out on big campus parties and fun, but I watched my son grow, and he watched me go on to achieve my degree.

In 1993, I walked across the stage in the Clarence M. Mitchell Jr. School of Engineering building on the campus of Morgan State University stage to receive my Bachelors Degree in electrical engineering for my son just as much as it was for me. I was happy that I persevered. My son gave me a reason everyday not to quit.

Below is a poem I read many years ago, but certain lines in the poem remain in my mind and keep me going when life gets overwhelming. Enjoy reading and commit what you need to memory, but whatever you do, just don't quit!

DON'T YOU QUIT
An Inspirational Poem -Author, unknown

>When things go wrong, as they sometimes will,
>
>When the road you're trudging seems all uphill,
>
>When the funds are low and the debts are high,
>
>And you want to smile, but you have to sigh,
>
>When care is pressing you down a bit-
>
>Rest if you must, but don't you quit.
>
>Life is queer with its twists and turns,
>
>As every one of us sometimes learns,
>
>And many a fellow turns about

When he might have won had he stuck it out.

Don't give up though the pace seems slow -

You may succeed with another blow.

Often the goal is nearer than

It seems to a faint and faltering man;

Often the struggler has given up

When he might have captured the victor's cup;

And he learned too late when the night came down,

How close he was to the golden crown.

Success is failure turned inside out -

The silver tint in the clouds of doubt,

And you never can tell how close you are,

It might be near when it seems afar;

So stick to the fight when you're hardest hit -

It's when things seem worst that you must not quit.

Exercise:

What dreams do you have for yourself? There are 4 categories listed below that can help you to get focused. Think about your life right now, where you are and where you want to go. Use the space below to write down at least 3 things that you desire in each area.

A) PERSONAL (this is what you want for you and only you)

1.

2.

3.

B) FAMILY (what you want for kids, parents, or what you want in a husband-to-be, or other family members)

1.

2.

3.

C) CAREER (this could be job, school, business or anything that will help you achieve your financial or personal growth goals)

1.

2.

3.

D) SPIRITUAL (what you want for your soul, salvation, spiritual strength...)

1.

2.

3.

You are worthy of your deepest desires, wants, wishes, dreams and goals!!!! God will show you how he can make your vision come to life! You can achieve anything if you just don't quit. Write down at least 3 reasons why you will not quit.

How To Become An UNSTOPPABLE Black Woman

Dear Black Woman:

Are you chasing your dreams? If not, why not? Now is the time, and today is the day to dig out dreams you've neatly packed away. You must put in motion things and ideas that are collecting dust as they sit and wait, and waste precious time on the shelf—in your mind. Life is like a shadow, a mist. It passes quickly by, and is no more. What are you doing with your life? Where is your passion? Where's your Joy?

You have some unfinished business that only you are fit to complete. Your ideas and dreams were given to you. You must move now, or you will waste precious time. *"Don't wait for the perfect moment. Take this moment and make it perfect."* You may say you need money. That may be true, but we have moved mountains with our will alone. You were born at the right time, at this time, for a specific purpose. Dust off your shoes, roll up your sleeves and get busy. You have a legacy to leave to your seed to the generations to come.

You have the power to take back anything that has slipped from your grasp. While you still have time, take back your life, your dreams, your health, your mind, your joy and your happiness. Don't worry about all the things you need, the things you may not have today, put your dreams on paper and get busy, don't delay. Did you ever hear "A roaring lion kills no game?" Let me help you understand - you cannot achieve or gain anything by mere sitting around and just talking about it.

Stand tall. Look people in the eye. Don't shrink out of view or be afraid of any person along the way. You are a blessing, God's one-of-a-kind creation. No one is greater than you. Don't be afraid of succeeding, you were born to succeed. Don't be afraid of failing either. J.K. Rowling said it best, "It is impossible to live without failing at something, unless you live so cautiously that you might as well not have lived at all, in which case you have failed by default."

You are here for a purpose. If you are unsure why you are here, just ask the Creator.

You have so much greatness in you! Your greatness and your creativity are begging to come out. Walk in your greatness. Let go of fear and release all doubt. Feed you mind things that build you up. Turn off, shut out, and say no to anything that does not support who you are or what you aspire to be. Do the same with your plate and with every drink in your cup. Let the things you take in to your body be for your benefit not to your detriment. Clear your mind of toxic thoughts and ideas. Strengthen the internal parts of you and you will be equipped to deal with the external forces around you.

You have an assignment to do and may be limited in days or years on this earth. Stand tall knowing you have everything in you to make your dreams come true. Others are depending on you to do what you have to do. Don't feed into lies, don't you dare sell your soul— not for a piece a paper, no amount of money, silver or gold.

Live to please God and to fulfill your part. You're resilient and brilliant and have been from the beginning. You are creative and gifted. You have no limits. Nothing can stop you. You aren't even limited by the sky. You are created in the image of the most High God!

Don't talk about what's wrong. Come up with a plan to change what is within your power. Be solution-oriented. When your time here on earth is over, will you be proud of what you have done? Don't you want to hear the Creator say, "Well done, my good and faithful servant.

Don't put your dreams on the shelf. Don't shrink back. Don't bury your gifts. That would be an insult. Whatever you do, don't hide from the sun (or the Son); it is our good friend because it activates the melanin that makes our beautiful black skin. It stirs up the gifts that are screaming to come out, it is the rhythm in our soul all the way down to the marrow in our bones.

Each day you rise, remember you have a choice. Choose one or the other, the choice is yours.

- Idea queen or implementation queen
- Worthless or worthwhile
- Pitiful or powerful
- Fearful or fearless
- Bitter or better

Don't let anything stop you from reaching your dreams. You are UNSTOPPABLE!

Love,

Tamlyn (an UNSTOPPABLE Black woman)

Notes

Chapter 1: I Got You!

1. "Commitment." *Merriam-Webster.com*. 2015. http://www.merriam-webster.com (17 November 2015).

2. "Compassion." *Merriam-Webster.com*. 2015. http://www.merriam-webster.com (17 November 2015).

3. "Compunction." *Merriam-Webster.com*. 2015. http://www.merriam-webster.com (17 November 2015).

4. "Compromise." *Merriam-Webster.com*. 2015. http://www.merriam-webster.com (17 November 2015).

5. "Cheerleader." *Merriam-Webster.com*. 2015. http://www.merriam-webster.com (17 November 2015).

6. "Constructive." *Merriam-Webster.com*. 2015. http://www.merriam-webster.com (17 November 2015).

7. Compatible." *Merriam-Webster.com*. 2015. http://www.merriam-webster.com (17 November 2015).

Chapter 3: Cherish Your Femininity

8. "gentleman." *Merriam-Webster.com*. 2015. http://www.merriam-webster.com (17 November 2015).

9. "lady." *Merriam-Webster.com*. 2015. http://www.merriam-webster.com (17 November 2015).

Made in the USA
Middletown, DE
13 March 2016